The SEVEN SORROWS of Mary

A Meditative Guide

In his reflective portrayal of the gifts of Mary of Sorrows, Giallanza shows her as a powerful model for our times. A profound meditation for readers of all faiths.

Sister Joy O'Grady, C.S.C.
President, Sisters of the Holy Cross

As a member of a religious community devoted to Mary as Our Sorrowful Mother, I am very familiar with reflections on Mary's seven sorrows. Yet I found fresh wisdom and new challenges in Brother Joel's book. He has presented these events in Mary's life in a way that calls us to reexamine the transforming power of the grace-filled events in our own lives.

Sister Ginny Silvestri
Prioress Provincial, Servants of Mary

The SEVEN SORROWS of Mary

A Meditative Guide

Joel Giallanza, C.S.C.

AVE MARIA PRESS AVE Notre Dame, Indiana

The scripture quotations contained herein are from the *New Revised Standard Version* Bible, copyright © 1989 by the Division of Christian Education of the National Council of the Churches of Christ in the U.S.A., and are used by permission. All rights reserved.

The quotation in the dedication is taken from *Christian Meditations* by Basil Moreau, C.S.C., Montreal: St. Joseph Oratory, 1932.

Founded in 1865, Ave Maria Press is a ministry of the United States Province of Holy Cross.

www.avemariapress.com

ISBN-10 1-59471-176-3   ISBN-13 978-1-59471-176-3

Cover and text design by John R. Carson.

Cover photo © Kamil Vojnar / Photonica.

Interior image © Brand X/SuperStock.

Printed and bound in the United States of America.

Library of Congress Cataloging-in-Publication Data

Giallanza, Joel.
  The seven sorrows of Mary : a meditative guide / Joel Giallanza.
     p. cm.
  ISBN-13: 978-1-59471-176-3 (pbk.)
  ISBN-10: 1-59471-176-3 (pbk.)
  1. Mary, Blessed Virgin, Saint--Meditations. I. Title.

  BT608.5.G53 2008
  232.91--dc22

                                2008013060

In honor of
Blessed Basil Anthony Moreau (1799–1873),
Founder of the Priests, Brothers, and Sisters of Holy Cross,
who challenges us to remain ever close to Mary.

We need to understand the effect produced in the heart of Mary by this sevenfold sword. To express it we would need to comprehend the tremendous love that Mary had for her Son, and her passionate desire and burning zeal for our salvation. No one could ever probe the depths of the love of the Mother of God for her Son as well as the no less incomprehensible love she has for us.

—*Christian Meditations*
Basil Moreau, C.S.C.

Contents

ACKNOWLEDGMENTS

However solitary an adventure writing a book may appear to be, it comes with a keen awareness of people and experiences that have made the writing possible. Such an awareness provides the perspective that a book's passage from concept to completion is more extensive than can be measured by the simple count of calendar days. I owe gratitude to many who have been a part of that passage for this book.

I am profoundly grateful to the Marianite Sisters of Holy Cross who first introduced me to Our Lady of Sorrows in a personal way and to the chaplet of the seven dolors. That introduction initiated a relationship with Mary that has remained a regular part of my spiritual practice and religious life.

Many people have listened to and offered suggestions on these reflections as they evolved and were used in retreats and days of reflection. Their support has truly influenced what the reader now holds, and I appreciate their generosity and kindness in providing comment and critique.

My brothers and sisters in Holy Cross continue to be an example and an inspiration to me in their devotion to Mary of Sorrows. I am grateful for the opportunity to write and share these reflections.

A special word of gratitude is due to Tom Grady, publisher at Ave Maria Press, and Bob Hamma, editorial director. They have been enthusiastic and encouraging about this project from the first time we met on the University of Notre Dame campus. Campbell Irving, as editor and participant in that first meeting, has been a valuable resource and gracious guide throughout the entire publication process. His recommendations and suggestions always reflected his editorial expertise and his genuine care for the quality of the project.

The final word of acknowledgment and gratitude must be reserved for Our Lady of Sorrows herself. Throughout the process of this writing Mary's presence and guidance have been evident to me in a variety of ways. If this book can be but a small part of making her better loved and known as a wise guide for the spiritual life, then it will serve a truly noble purpose.

THE WOMAN
AND THE SWORD:

A Story

Quietly, she walked away from the tomb; there was nothing more to do here. Besides, the Sabbath was fast approaching. Time to go home.

"Home? I wonder where that is?" the woman asked. Her thoughts wandered back to images of a young girl with an ancient promise. She was to be the mother of a son who would fulfill God's promise of freedom and new life. It was told her that she would be remembered for ages upon ages.

And now? Now she walks away from the tomb where she just placed that son. Friends say it might be better if she came with them into hiding for a few days. As she had done so many times over the years, the woman pondered . . . then she remembered. . . .

She didn't really know anything about swords. Oh, she had seen the Romans with all their military hardware—they were impossible to miss! And swords were even part of her own people's history. To become a people and to claim a land involved wars, and wars meant swords. But her people were victorious; of course, God promised that. "Even more," the woman thought, "the scriptures tell us we are 'a people saved by the Lord, the shield of your help, and the sword of your triumph!'" (Dt 33:29). Yes, the woman had seen and heard about swords, but always from a distance. And that was fine with her.

The woman first met the sword after the birth of her son. To be exact, it was introduced to her the very day she brought him for ritual presentation in the temple. A holy man, Simeon, was in the temple just then and said some amazing things about her son. What caught her attention in particular were the ominous words he directed toward her: "A sword will pierce your own soul, too" (Lk 2:35). "A sword will pierce me because of my son?" she thought. Unsettling words to say the least on such a joyous occasion! She wondered, "How can I defend my son and myself unless I wield a sword?" It was as if she had spoken out loud. At that point, Anna, a woman who was always in the temple, "began to praise God and to speak about the child to all who were looking for the redemption of Jerusalem" (Lk 2:38). Then Anna said to the woman, "The sword is not yours to possess, but only to experience." When all the rituals were completed, the woman and her son and her husband went home. The woman pondered . . . and believed. . . .

The woman was stunned, as if out of breath from a piercing punch. Her husband had just awakened her and spoken words of horror: "King Herod has ordered the male children to be killed." Swords again. Instinctively, she picked up her son and encircled him within the strength and safety of her arms. Her husband continued, "I was told to 'take the child and his mother, and flee to Egypt, and remain there until I tell you'" (Mt 2:13). The woman knew the escape would have to begin now, during the night, before dawn's light could mark their path. She quickly gathered the few things they needed. The force of her husband's words struck fear within her each time she heard them. Anxious thoughts raced through her. "This will not be an easy journey, especially with the baby. God, help us!" Her husband gestured that their simple transport was ready. The woman held her son; her husband led the way. For a while, every sound on the road caused her arms to tighten around her child. Then the journey seemed safely underway, to a place far away. The woman pondered . . . and loved. . . .

"I haven't seen him." The words were repeated by relatives and friends. The woman's son was not in the caravan, and a day of travel had already passed. There was no alternative; she and her husband would have to retrace their steps and return to the city. They wondered, "He's a little boy in a big city, where are we going to look?" Concern cut through the woman's heart like a sword. The search began as soon as they departed the caravan. By the third day, fearful and frustrated and fatigued, the woman and her husband went to pray. As they entered the temple, "they found him, sitting among the teachers, listening to them, and asking them questions" (Lk 2:46). The woman spoke directly, "Why have you treated us like this? Look, your father and I have been searching for you in great anxiety" (Lk 2:48). The boy's response about needing to be in his father's house could just as well have been in another language. The woman did not understand. The boy obediently went home with his parents. The woman pondered . . . and hoped. . . .

There were always images and stories about Roman crucifixion, each more terrorizing than the last. But none of them prepared the woman for what she saw in today's spectacle. The parade of death and the pallor of her son were far beyond even the most exaggerated stories she had been told. As he passed, every muscle in her body tensed, prepared to reach out and hold him. But glistening Roman swords assured the pace of the parade and the passivity of passersby. The sting of her tears reflected her helplessness. Yes, the woman knew her son had done and said things that were controversial; she knew he had not endeared himself to the authorities. Still, she did not think she would ever be standing here, on the street that winds and climbs its way to the Skull Place. Walking with the "great number of the people following him" (Lk 23:27), she could hear the wondering whispers drifting her way, "Isn't that his mother?" She watched and walked and followed. The woman pondered . . . and believed and loved and hoped. . . .

"Woman, here is your son" (Jn 19:26), was all he said. Her eyes met those of the young man standing next to her, realizing he was the one being referred to. "Here is your mother" (Jn 19:27), was all he said to the young man. She knew these words gave his followers the responsibility of continuing his filial duties. It was the custom. Her future life would be in their company, beginning at this place of death. Now, time could not be halted; the woman's son was dying and she could but stand at the foot of his cross, waiting and watching and wondering. "Would his death mean anything? Why is this happening? Would anyone remember his life, the words he spoke, the good he did?" The stream of her wonderments was interrupted by his voice, "It is finished" (Jn 19:30), was all he said. And truly it was. The tinkle of Roman swords as the soldiers gathered their instruments and prepared to return to the city signaled to her the conclusion of this death-watch. Her son was dead. The woman pondered . . . and believed. . . .

He was so beautiful when first she held him. But now. . . . All the confusion and uncertainty and wonderment accompanying her pregnancy when first she held him evaporated. But now. . . . The woman experienced then what all mothers experience, the mystery and the majesty of life. But now, that was more than thirty years ago. The body she now held—broken and battered—resembled almost nothing of the child she knew, of the child first handed to her by another Joseph in another time. The woman held her son and wept; pain pierced and probed her heart with the precision of a well-honed sword. She had this opportunity because a member of the Council, Joseph by name, "went to Pilate and asked for the body of Jesus. Then he took it down" (Lk 23:52–53). The woman held her son and wept. There was nothing else to do. The woman pondered . . . and loved. . . .

Joseph, the one from Arimathaea, did not agree with the Council's decision to seek this man's death. His protest was not even discussed. Now, he approached the woman, took the body, "wrapped it in a linen cloth, and laid it in a rock-hewn tomb where no one had ever been laid" (Lk 23:53). "Thank you," the woman said, "I will not forget your kindness." Joseph spoke softly, "The Council made its decision, and I made mine. He will be buried with dignity." The woman lingered near the shrouded body; she heard Joseph's soft voice, "We have to go, Sabbath light is coming." He led her out of the tomb, then rolled a stone across the entrance. With the thump of the stone's settling, the woman felt the sword strike, deep in the heart, where hope dwells. The woman pondered . . . and hoped. . . .

The woman had remembered. . . . Now, quietly, she walked away from the tomb; there was nothing more to do here. Besides, the Sabbath was fast approaching. Time to go home. . . . It was told her that she would be remembered for ages upon ages.

"LOOK AND SEE"

Many have traveled along the pathways of the spiritual life, following the pattern established by Jesus and confirmed by a countless multitude of holy people since his death and resurrection, even to our own day. Most have passed by unnoticed, faithful to God through their everyday tasks and responsibilities, some even heroically so, but still unknown by the standards of distinction in history. It has been for family and friends to note their heroism and holiness. Others have walked those same pathways with similar fidelity, but by God's grace and through their time and place in history, they have become models and guides for many others, and have remained so for centuries after their death. Among the most outstanding models and guides stands a simple Jewish woman about whom we have precious few details: Mary of Nazareth.

Mary has been and continues to be celebrated and honored under a variety of titles, reflecting the extraordinary diversity and wonderful richness of people and societies, cultures and ethnic groups around the world. All of those titles can be summed up eloquently by the three words that designate Mary's greatest distinction: Mother of God. The wide range of manifestations under which Mary is honored testifies to her attractiveness as a wise companion for the spiritual life and her accessibility as an experienced guide along its pathways. It is no surprise, then, that a broad spectrum of devotions to Mary has developed over the course of two thousand years. And still others are emerging.

The most familiar devotion, the Rosary, provides a panorama of graced events in the lives and experiences of Jesus and Mary, highlighting and celebrating the good news of the Incarnation, the Paschal Mystery, and our salvation by God's gracious design. Though it traces its Christian roots to the second, third, and fifteenth centuries, even this ancient devotion has evolved. In 2002 Pope John Paul II expanded the Rosary by adding the Luminous Mysteries to the already well-known Joyful, Sorrowful, and Glorious ones.

Mary of Sorrows

Another devotion and title that gives us a glimpse into the person and perspective of Mary are her sorrows. The origins of the liturgical feast of Our Lady of Sorrows reach back to the early sixteenth century when Pope Julius II proposed a feast honoring Mary's sufferings. The theological mood of the time, however, considered the notion that Mary could be grief-stricken as irreverent. Subsequently, Julius did not pursue his proposal. Nothing further was heard of the feast until the late seventeenth century when the Friar Servants of Mary (popularly known as the Servites) initiated the feast locally in Italy because of their devotion to the sufferings of Mary. Pope Pius VII officially established the feast for the whole church in 1814 in thanksgiving for his return to Rome after being held captive in France for several years by Napoleon. Early in the twentieth century, Saint Pius X designated September 15 as the annual celebration of the feast. In art, Our Lady of Sorrows is most often depicted with seven swords piercing her heart.

Mary of Sorrows and the Religious of Holy Cross

In 1835 Blessed Basil Moreau, a priest of the Diocese of Le Mans, France, founded a group known as the Auxiliary Priests to preach missions and assist in parishes that were still recovering from the aftereffects of the French Revolution. In that same year, he was appointed as superior of the Brothers of Saint Joseph, a group of laymen founded fifteen years earlier to assist in educational and pastoral ministries that were struggling similarly. Two years later he united these groups into a single association and settled them in that section of Le Mans known as *Sainte-Croix* (Holy Cross). These brothers and priests eventually developed into the religious community known as the Congregation of (or from) Holy Cross. With the founding of the sisters in 1841, Moreau realized his vision and plan to establish a single community of men and women dedicated to the service of the Church. The patroness of the locale where all this developed was Our Lady of Holy Cross, who is depicted as Our Lady of the Seven Dolors (or Sorrows).

As the religious family of Holy Cross began to grow and develop Moreau's desire was that the three groups remain ever united in heart and mind in their commitment to identify with Jesus and continue his mission. Fr. Moreau wrote to the members of the community in 1844,

> It is this perfect unity which, with the aid of grace, I have tried to cement by consecrating the priests to the Sacred Heart of Jesus, the brothers to the Most Pure Heart of Joseph, and the sisters to the Immaculate Heart of Mary. . . . I hereby order each and every one . . . to fast on

> the vigils of the Sacred Heart, Our Lady of the Seven Dolors, and the feast of Saint Joseph. I desire these three feasts to be observed with all possible solemnity. (Circular Letter 20)

In 1857, when the conventual church of the mother house in Le Mans was completed, it was consecrated and dedicated to the honor of Our Lady of Holy Cross. After the consecration on June 16, the feast of the dedication was celebrated annually in November to coincide with the feast of the dedication of the basilica of Saint John Lateran in Rome. This, then, became the principal feast for the men's congregation. The sisters continued to celebrate Our Lady of Sorrows as their principal feast.

In 1920 the congregation of priests and brothers formally designated Our Lady of Sorrows, celebrated on September 15, as the patronal feast. Today, this remains a principal feast for the four religious congregations within the Family of Holy Cross; the Sisters of the Holy Cross also celebrate September 14, the Exaltation of the Holy Cross, as their particular patronal feast.

Father Moreau himself always had a lively devotion to Mary, beginning in his childhood. Our Lady of Sorrows had special appeal for him because of the high priority given to the place of the cross in his spirituality, and to the importance of identifying with Jesus through one's personal experiences of the cross. That devotion and appeal constitute a part of Moreau's legacy and are evident even today among Holy Cross religious. Our spiritual relationship with Mary is essentially apostolic. Because she accompanied Jesus through these painful experiences, we can turn to her with confidence for support and encouragement as we accompany others through difficult moments in their lives. Like her, we are willing to stand at the foot of the cross and share in the suffering of others. We hope to be, as she was, an example of compassion and love for others.

Mary remains with Jesus through his passion and shares in his sufferings. She is present when he dies. Mary is a model of faithfulness in the midst of confusion, darkness, and pain. She is a sign of the promise of new life that is borne from the cross. Mary of Sorrows is a living example of the motto of the Family of Holy Cross: *Spes Unica*—the cross is our only hope. As people of the cross, we in the congregation must be people with hope to bring to our world. For Father Moreau, this was the challenge that Mary of Sorrows placed before all of us.

The Sorrows

Traditionally, seven sorrows of Mary are recognized. They are rooted in stories from the gospel narratives, though not all seven are mentioned explicitly. They focus on events and experiences in Mary's life that were difficult and painful, giving her a direct share in the Paschal Mystery of her son. The seven sorrows are: Hearing Simeon's prophecy as Jesus was presented in the temple; Making the urgent trip to Egypt in response to King Herod's death threat; Losing Jesus in the temple when he was twelve years old; Accompanying Jesus on the journey to Calvary; Being with Jesus during the crucifixion; Receiving the dead body of Jesus; and Burying Jesus.

"Is it nothing to you, all you who pass by? Look and see if there is any sorrow like my sorrow, which was brought upon me, which the Lord inflicted" (Lam 1:12). Though it refers to the devastation of Jerusalem, this text is well suited for a woman who has experienced all these things in her life. Mary of Nazareth was familiar with suffering; she had encountered the cross in her own life long before that day on Calvary. Even on that day, her faith, love, and hope remained firmly anchored in God. Years before, Mary had already proclaimed the response that would mark her entire life: "Here am I, the servant of the Lord; let it be with me according to your word" (Lk 1:38).

This is a response she lived and passed on to others. At the wedding in Cana, while referring to Jesus, Mary says to the servants, "Do whatever he tells you" (Jn 2:5). These are Mary's last recorded words in the gospel. As she did, so she taught others to do. Her life resounds with the words of her son: "If any want to become my followers, let them deny themselves and take up their cross and follow me" (Lk 9:23). The words of the son are first fulfilled in the life of his mother. "Look and see."

The Temple and the Journey

Even though the events on which these reflections will focus transpired more than two millennia ago, there is wisdom to be learned from Mary's response to them, wisdom that can be a guide for us in our spiritual lives. Like Mary, we will encounter the cross. If we choose to follow Jesus, to be in relationship with Jesus, then there is no other way. The road to new life necessarily goes through the cross. Our own sufferings and sorrows may not be at all similar to those that Mary encountered; nevertheless, the example of her life and response in those experiences can strengthen and encourage us as we confront the cross.

The paradigm to be used for exploring the richness of Mary's sorrows is already evident in several of these seven events: the temple and the journey. Both of these are arenas for encountering God's presence and activity in the spiritual life. They form a weaving and reflect the dynamic progression that marks the process of transformation as we move toward union with God. The temple is a place for listening to God's words and learning God's ways; the journey provides the pathways we need to love and to live all that we hear from God and learn of God.

Mary has much to teach us about listening and learning, loving and living. And so we begin. This is Mary's story, her journey from the birth to the death of her Son; and even beyond, for she is still with us. This is Mary of Sorrows. Look and See.

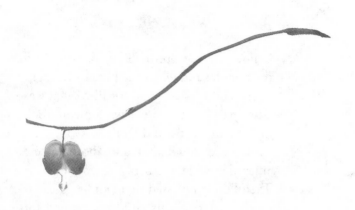

"A Sword Will
Pierce Your Own
Soul, Too"

THE FIRST SORROW

> Guided by the Spirit, Simeon came into the temple; and when the parents brought in the child Jesus, to do for him what was customary under the law, Simeon took him in his arms and praised God. . . . And the child's father and mother were amazed at what was being said about him. Then Simeon blessed them and said to his mother Mary, "This child is destined for the falling and the rising of many in Israel, and to be a sign that will be opposed so that the inner thoughts of many will be revealed—and a sword will pierce your own soul, too." (Lk 2:27–28, 33–35)

The temple, a sacred space, a place filled with God's presence and, in this scene, it is meant to be a place of joy. The reason behind this story was a common occurrence, proud parents bringing their first-born son to be presented to God as the Mosaic Law required. Once the blessing was given and the rituals completed, the family would return home to celebrate the new life with which

they had been blessed. It is indeed a time of great joy—
under usual circumstances. Mary's experience on this day,
however, moves in a different direction. She is confronted
with an ominous prophecy and a promise of future pain,
indicating decisions that will have to be made in the years
ahead.

An elder among the people, a person of insight, a
"righteous and devout" man, Simeon by name, greets the
parents as they enter the temple and takes the child in
his arms. He praises God and prophesies that this child
is indeed the "salvation which you have prepared in the
presence of all peoples" (Lk 2:30–31). After the custom-
ary blessing of the parents, Simeon addresses Mary in
words that are less than comforting. He refers to her son
as "a sign that will be opposed," and he tells her that "a
sword will pierce your own soul, too." What began as a
moment of joy has now changed into a time of confusion
and concern.

The Sword

In the fourteenth chapter of Ezekiel, the prophet is
reprimanding those who have been unfaithful to God
through idolatry. He insists that God's judgments upon
them will be particularly severe because all have suc-
cumbed to the seductions of idolatry's empty promises. In
describing one of those judgments through the prophet,

God says, "If I bring a sword upon that land and say, 'Let a sword pass through the land,' and I cut off human beings and animals from it; though these three men were in it, as I live, says the Lord God . . . they alone would be saved" (14:17–18). The "three men" being referred to are Noah, Daniel, and Job as outstanding examples of the integrity and fidelity necessary to maintain an intimate relationship with God even in the face of tempting alternatives. The sword that strikes here is the sword of distinction separating those who are faithful from those who are not. This is the sword to which Simeon refers.

Jesus' own life and mission will be marked by this sword. In describing his presence and activity, he is uncompromising: "Do not think that I have come to bring peace to the earth; I have not come to bring peace, but a sword" (Mt 10:34). Simeon has prophesied the very sign that Jesus' life and mission will be. Jesus is God's own word, and that word "is living and active, sharper than any two-edged sword, piercing until it divides soul from spirit, joints from marrow; it is able to judge the thoughts and intentions of the heart" (Heb 4:12). This same sword slices through Mary's heart as Jesus' future is unveiled on this day in the temple. It will slice again as that future unfolds in the coming years.

Mary must choose to embrace this sword even as she will be called to embrace Jesus' message and mission with all the turbulence they will inevitably bring. This choice must be her own because neither family ties nor familiarity with Jesus are sure guarantees for faith. Mary is unquestionably a woman of integrity, a model of fidelity. Her response to the Annunciation had already heralded a path that would draw her progressively deeper into the Paschal Mystery. This scene at the temple is but one point along the way that God is leading her.

The Challenge

Simeon's prophecy gives Mary a glimpse into the meaning of Jesus' life. That same prophecy reveals to us the meaning of life for all those who are committed to the spiritual life, for living and working and loving as Jesus did. Such a commitment situates us at the cutting edge of life and death, truth and falsehood, decisiveness and passivity, passion and apathy. With Mary, our soul and spirit and self-image will be pierced by our relationship with Jesus, revealing either the integrity or inconsistency between what we profess to be and what we actually do.

Like Mary we too must choose to embrace what God asks of us; we must choose to embrace Jesus' example for our own lives. The choice must be made and it must be a personal decision because faith and fidelity cannot be assumed and they surely cannot be feigned, at least not for very long. We cannot know in advance the precise pathways along which our spiritual lives will take us. This is a blessing, whether or not we perceive it as such, because we might be tempted to customize and control the configuration of those pathways, not allowing much room for God's presence and activity. If we are willing to follow the pathways that God opens before us, then, like Mary, we will encounter the sword of distinction.

The temple is a place of offering, a place for dedicating our lives to God. This first of Mary's sorrows proposes a challenge for our spiritual lives: we must offer to God that which is most valuable to us. Mary's example demonstrates a two-fold offering. She offered her entire life to God at the Annunciation. Now she offers the life of her son. This complete offering of self and of all that is most valuable constitutes the meaning of the Christian life and the means for rooting personal identity in Jesus and in his teaching. Such an offering must be evident in the lives of all those who profess to be his followers.

In our spiritual lives, we assign meaning to events and experiences and even objects. This is a natural and necessary process that affords us a way of prioritizing the materials, moments, and memories that fill our lives. And this same process provides us with a means for determining and distinguishing between what is prominent and permanent for our continued spiritual development, and what is peripheral and passing. Meaning shapes our identity for the present and for the future. When something has value and meaning for the way we choose to live, we create and maintain space and time and energy for it. Because we identify with it in some way, we sense that our lives would be less full without it. Over time, others recognize us, at least in part, by our identification with the realities that have meaning in our lives.

Offering what is most valuable assumes that we know the meaning of what we offer. If that offering is to be marked by integrity and sincerity, then it must come from our heart; it must be part of the very soil in which our heart is planted. Our faith calls us to situate God at the foundation of all that has meaning in our lives; we must root our identity in God alone. God must be the soil in which we grow.

We are created in God's image and likeness; God is the core and completion of our identity. We thus have the capacity for God. Whenever we assign value and meaning to realities that are marginal and momentary, we distort our vision of who and what we are as creatures of a loving God. Jesus reminds us, "where your treasure is, there your heart will be also" (Lk 12:34). We must take care, then, where we settle our heart, where we allow it to take root, so its treasure will be truly worthy of the God who created us, whose image and likeness we bear.

Mary's Example

The first of Mary's sorrows has led her to the temple, into the presence of God. Her example here teaches us that only from our deepest self, from our heart, can we offer to God what is most valuable. All else is secondary. She teaches us that the offering must be made, even when the consequences might be unpleasant or altogether unknown. We must offer our lives as Mary offered her own years before when she said, "let it be with me according to your word" (Lk 1:38). That offering has brought her to this day in the temple and to this encounter with the sword.

Our spiritual lives will be hindered or hastened, depending upon the quality of what we offer. If we present to God only peripheral aspects of our lives that we have designated as expendable, then our spiritual lives will develop erratically and intermittently with no consistent progress evident. Growth lies in offering all of life. Like Mary, we too will hear words or have experiences that reveal Jesus as the Promised One for us, the One to whom we must offer everything. The sword challenges us to faith and fidelity. The sword awaits our response.

☙ For Reflection ☙

To accept God's word and work in her life, Mary had to listen, even when what she heard was confusing or unclear. God does and will speak to us also, and, as it was for Mary, what is said to us may not be immediately discernible. We must listen attentively because God's word comes to us in many ways along various paths.

What is most helpful to me in listening for the word and to the word in my daily life?

How do I know and confirm that what I have heard is God's word in a particular situation or experience?

What must I yet do to be increasingly open to God's word in my life?

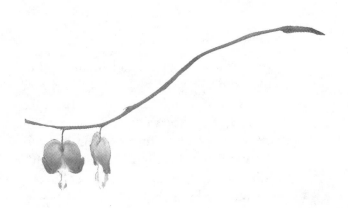

"Take the Child
and His Mother,
and Flee to Egypt"

THE SECOND SORROW

After (the wise men) had left, an angel of the Lord appeared to Joseph in a dream and said, "Get up, take the child and his mother, and flee to Egypt, and remain there until I tell you; for Herod is about to search for the child, to destroy him." Then Joseph got up, took the child and his mother by night, and went to Egypt, and remained there until the death of Herod. This was to fulfill what had been spoken by the Lord through the prophet, "Out of Egypt I have called my son." (Mt 2:13–15)

After the experience in the temple, a journey awaits Mary. This is an urgent journey, a hurried flight, impelled by the threat of death. In stark contrast to all the events surrounding the joyful announcement of birth and new life, darkness and death now loom on the horizon. Under usual circumstances, there would be a peacefulness and contentment in relishing this birth and the promise it heralds. But any delay in travel at this point could be disastrous. Joseph does what he is told; he takes his family and heads southwest to Egypt, far from Herod's jurisdiction. This is a journey from death to life; it would be a fatal mistake to underestimate its importance and necessity.

The rigors of the journey undertaken here, especially with a very young child, go far beyond mere inconvenience. The reason demanding this travel only compounds those rigors, intensifying them, making them frightening and dangerous. As a counterpoint, love and concern accent this scene from Saint Matthew's Gospel. Mary, Jesus, and Joseph are united to safeguard life, to survive. Mary makes this journey with loving trust that the angel's message in Joseph's dream will assure safe passage for her family. In responding to this call from God, she lives the words of the psalmist: "Hear, O daughter, consider and incline your ear; forget your people and your father's house, and the king will desire your beauty" (Ps 45:10–11). Once again Mary feels the edge of the sword.

The Sword

The means through which Mary now encounters the sword is no one less than King Herod. The reign of Herod the Great extended from 37 BC until 4 BC, though he is associated with the period that includes the early years of

Jesus' life. As a ruler, he was consistently concerned about and obsessively preoccupied with the security of his position as king and his ability to maintain possession of the throne. The story in which he orders the killing of "all the children in and around Bethlehem who were two years old or under, according to the time he had learned from the wise men" (Mt 2:16), gives us but one scene in the extensive violence that characterized his reign. He constructed his political security by imprisoning or slaughtering any who threatened his position, whether those threats were real or perceived.

Mary's maternal instinct and responsibility to protect her son's life from the oppressive and deadly designs of an insecure ruler place her in the mainstream of Jesus' mission. She will be a pioneer in the new exodus out of Egypt by which Jesus will lead the people into the new life of God's reign. To accomplish that, however, Mary must make this journey from the familiar and safe surroundings of Bethlehem to the unknown territories of Egypt. This trip is as necessary as it is urgent; it is a journey for life.

The sword of distinction now urges Mary to move, to travel, even though the road ahead is unknown and uncertain. Her union with Jesus here is particularly significant. That union during this journey will secure Jesus' life in the face of forces that seek to destroy it. Also, Mary's union with Jesus affirms her conviction about the mission that has been entrusted to her and assures her that, as before, the angel's instructions are worthy of her complete confidence and trust. This union does not dissipate the unknown and uncertain future that awaits this family, but it does confirm their resolve not to hesitate in setting out on the road before them.

The Challenge

Our spiritual journey, like Mary's own, can lead us from the familiar to the unknown. In fact, this is inevitable as we are drawn deeper into the life of God and the mission of Jesus. The sword of distinction challenges us not to retreat from the unknown that lies ahead, but to continue on our way as a demonstration of our love for Jesus. Accepting that challenge requires union with Christ. He must be our response to fear, our reason for trust, and our resolve to love. As it was for Mary, so it must be for us: Jesus must remain the design for and the direction of the spiritual life.

The sword will transform our lives, and therein is the challenge. We must move in the direction of the transformation. Now that her son was born and growing, Mary might have looked forward to settling down in the familiar routine that marked the life of many first-century wives and mothers. But her second sorrow shows us that quiet moments are replaced by quick maneuvers, and familiar terrain is left behind for a future of uncertainty.

With her husband and young son, she becomes a refugee. Decisions have to be made and actions have to be taken with clarity and speed. In such circumstances, movement assures life; hesitation invites death. The journey is not an option, but an obligation.

Such is the challenge before us. The spiritual life does not fare well on automatic pilot; we need to keep moving forward, to be pro-active concerning growth and development in our relationship with God. What is familiar and known to us, over time, becomes comforting and comfortable; sometimes, even when we know a particular change or adjustment would be beneficial for our lives, we stand still. We become immobile in an effort to secure and solidify what we have accomplished thus far. Future horizons may hold little appeal for us. Gradually, and eventually, that immobility leads us to believe that nothing more needs to be done.

Immobility is not security for the spiritual life, though we might be tempted to believe that it will safeguard our progress to date. In truth, such immobility drains us of passion for the journey; it fosters complacency, which feeds on the assumption that what we have experienced thus far is sufficient. This perspective gradually gives way to the conviction that any continuing efforts would have only minimal influence on our growth and development. Sufficiency in the spiritual life is but a thin camouflage for pride that erodes what has been accomplished for the present and disrupts whatever could nurture progress for the future.

The journey from this potential death will have to be made if we value our spiritual lives. The journey will unsettle our routines and lead us in unfamiliar and unknown directions. Even more, the journey will involve a process in which we gradually have less control over our own lives. We can easily articulate many reasons for hesitating to take even the first step on such a journey. That it is a movement from death and not to death can seem unclear. Self-preservation presents itself as the way that common sense would indicate to us to act. But Jesus alerts us, "Those who want to save their life will lose it, and those who lose their life for my sake will find it" (Mt 16:25). That we do not have sufficient resources, within ourselves, for self-preservation and self-advancement in the spiritual life is not always an easy lesson to learn. But we must learn it in one way or another, now or later, if we truly desire and choose to continue the journey.

Mary's Example

The second of Mary's sorrows has taken her on a journey from death to life. Her example here demonstrates that an intimate union with Jesus is intrinsic to progress in the spiritual life. Even more, that union is essential if the spiritual life is to exist and flourish at all. Union is a grace, but it is also a choice we must make in responding to that grace. It will sustain us on the journey even at the most difficult junctures. Mary teaches us to make the choice, regardless of what lies ahead. "Before each person are life and death, and whichever one chooses will be given" (Sir 15:17). Mary's choice is clearly evident.

The spiritual life is dynamic by nature—at least it is meant to be. It can become static and eventually stagnant because of the choices that we make. Like Mary, we too will be compelled to travel from a well-known and comfortable environment to a new place in which God's grace will be our only compass. The sword challenges us to confidence and trust. Once again, the sword awaits our response.

৶   For Reflection   ৶

To protect what was most precious to her, Mary had to make decisions and choices that would safeguard not only the life of her son, but also the mission that God had entrusted to her. Social forces and personal habits can distort and even diminish the values and priorities by which we want to live. We must safeguard whatever realities are essential for our continuing spiritual growth.

Given my daily life and responsibilities, what are the top five priorities by which I live?

What spiritual practices assist me in monitoring and maintaining those priorities?

What are the greatest challenges for my fidelity to the spiritual life, and how do I respond to those challenges?

"THEY DID NOT
FIND HIM"

THE THIRD SORROW

Now every year Jesus' parents went to Jerusalem for the festival of the Passover. And when he was twelve years old, they went up as usual for the festival. When the festival was ended and they started to return, the boy Jesus stayed behind in Jerusalem, but his parents did not know it. Assuming that he was in the group of travelers, they went a day's journey. Then they started to look for him among their relatives and friends. When they did not find him, they returned to Jerusalem to search for him. After three days they found him in the temple sitting among the teachers, listening to them and asking them questions. . . . When his parents saw him they were astonished; and his mother said to him, "Child, why have you treated us like this? Look, your father and I have been searching for you in great anxiety." He said to them, "Why were you searching for me? Did you not know that I must be in my Father's house?" But they did not understand what he said to them. (Lk 2:41–46, 48–50)

This scene unfolds during a festive time of year, a celebration of liberation. Jewish law mandated an annual pilgrimage to Jerusalem for each of several important feasts. Because of the potential economic hardship that mandate could present, an exception was made for those who lived far away from the city. They were required to make the pilgrimage only at Passover. Typically, extended families traveled together in caravans, to share resources, enjoy one another's company, and provide a safe environment on the open road. For a twelve-year-old boy, this was an adventure, a time to get away from the limited confines of his small village. There were many sights to see along the way and in the city, solemn temple services to attend, stories of earlier pilgrimages to hear, various foods to enjoy, places to pray and play, and souvenirs to purchase.

Since Jesus was yet one year away from official adulthood, which began at thirteen years of age, he probably had more free time than his elders to explore the city and the temple. Even though he had been to Jerusalem in previous years, there would always be new places to see and familiar sites to revisit. It is not hard to imagine a twelve-year-old boy losing track of time in such circumstances. On the return trip, as the caravan makes its way back to Nazareth, the festive mood of Mary and Joseph and their relatives and friends must have been displaced by panic once it was confirmed, after an initial day of searching the caravan, that Jesus was not among them. The sword appears in Mary's life again.

The Sword

Her young son's fascination with Jerusalem and the temple is the means through which Mary now encounters the sword. Most, if not all, parents of preteens could engage Mary in conversation about this incident and discover that there is much common ground in their experiences. Given the security with which we strive to surround children, contemporary readers may find it more than curious that Mary and Joseph depart Jerusalem "assuming that (Jesus) was in the group of travelers" with them. There is no parental irresponsibility here. In a tribal culture, every member of an extended family shares responsibility for the children. Mary and Joseph would have assumed, appropriately, that Jesus had been informed about the departure day and time. The decision to return to the city comes after they realize that the cultural assumption had not been reliable in this instance.

Mary's journey involves separation from her son. To proceed, she must be detached, not from Jesus, but from everything except Jesus. She must proceed in hope, so she searches, first among family and friends and other traveling companions. When that effort brings no results, she leaves the security of the caravan and retraces her steps back to the city. The decision to turn around, no doubt, was filled with concern for her son and with anxiety and fear about what she would discover. The gospel does not tell us if Mary and Joseph made this return trip alone or if others offered to go with them. In either case, the festivities of the preceding days must have seemed but a dream of the distant past.

Three days pass before mother and son are reunited. Eventually and inevitably Mary and Joseph make their way to the temple—the center of religious and cultural life. Does their search lead them to this holy place because the people to whom they had spoken recalled seeing Jesus in or around the temple area? Did the futility of their efforts and the fatigue of their search direct them to prayer and petition before God because they simply did not know what else to do or where to turn? The story does not provide us with any material for possible answers to such questions. Nevertheless, when Mary and Joseph do arrive at the temple, they find Jesus there, "sitting among the teachers, listening to them and asking them questions." As it would be with most parents, their experience at that moment may have been a mixture of relief, annoyance, and wonderment.

The Challenge

This experience in the temple contrasts the earlier one, the first of Mary's encounters with the sword. Then, the temple was the setting for a moment of joy, but tinged with sorrow by an ominous prophecy. Now it is a place where the anxious hearts of weary parents are lightened with joy and relief upon locating their son. This joy and relief, however, are not without points to be pondered. In response to Mary's request for an explanation of his actions, Jesus responds with questions of his own. "Why were you searching for me? Did you not know that I must be in my Father's house?" Jesus' questions reflect surprise that his parents would not have determined quickly his whereabouts in the city. It is as if he is asking, "Where else would I be?"

In this third of Mary's sorrows, the challenge is to recognize and accept the quest for Jesus as a substantive dimension of our Christian life and mission. Mary is the pioneer of this quest and so models the spiritual life for us. Admittedly, our own life and mission cannot replicate exactly Mary's own; each person's spiritual life and relationship with God will unfold in a unique way, even though there will be some common elements in the lives of all Christians. Among those common elements is the commitment to seek and find Jesus in whatever experiences our lives may present to us. Such a commitment confirms the integrity of our desire and efforts to follow him.

Our spiritual lives will bring us to periods during which we experience the absence of Jesus, times when we look for evidence of Jesus' presence and activity in all the familiar and expected dimensions of our lives and yet do not find him. These periods and times place us at a crossroads. We could take the road of discouragement and despair, in which case we would find no incentive for expending further time and energy to maintain the spiritual life. The sword, however, cuts a path along the road of detachment and hope. Like Mary, we will have to look for Jesus wherever our search leads us. If we fear moving beyond what is known and certain and secure, then our search will falter from our lack of effort and willingness to explore. With detachment and hope, our search will bring us to the temple, to the truth that Jesus is the only solid ground in which we must root our lives.

Our mission in life, our quest for Jesus, challenges us to reach beyond the narrow boundaries that we have established for our spiritual lives and to see more than the limited horizons inherent in our own assumptions and perspectives. To move outside those boundaries and horizons we will need the support of others, we will need to enter into relationships with them to learn about their experiences, to hear their stories, to seek their insight and wisdom. Those relationships are a valuable support, for our spiritual lives do not exist in isolation from the people, circumstances, and events surrounding us. The support that others provide can guide us in moving past the boundaries and horizons of self, opening us to vistas where God awaits us.

As we benefit from the support and assistance of others, so we can be of benefit to them in their spiritual life. This mutual and generous service becomes a reflection of God's loving presence and activity in our world. Like Mary, then, our own mission has a share in the mission of Jesus himself. Ultimately, our search for Jesus does not end in some discovery that brings a definitive close to all that we had experienced beforehand. Rather, our search leads us, as did Mary's own, to the "Father's house," to a way of life in union with Jesus.

Mary's Example

The third of Mary's sorrows has brought her on a quest and led her to the temple. Her example demonstrates for us that our longing to be united with Jesus will guide us in ways that are unexpected and, at times, even unwelcome at least as far as our preferences may be concerned. We might prefer the spiritual life to move along smoothly with no surprises. But there can be no guarantees for that if we are truly committed to following wherever the Holy Spirit leads us. After her discovery of and dialogue with

Jesus, Mary "treasured all these things in her heart" (Lk 2:51). We will have to do the same.

Our spiritual lives progress by discernment and discovery in response to God's grace. We will need to be faithful and we will need to be patient because the way before us may not always be well defined, and the time line will be God's and not ours to determine. Mary treasured all that she experienced; the Scriptures do not tell us that she understood all that took place in her life. But it was cherished as valuable for her relationship with God. So, too, the sword challenges us to live from the heart, to treasure and to live whatever God asks of us, without always understanding. The sword awaits our response.

⌒ࣷ For Reflection ⌒ࣷ

To be close to Jesus, to find him when distance separated them, Mary had to look and long for him; she had
to take some practical steps to locate him. God is present
and active in our lives at all times; nevertheless, there
will be moments when we do not sense that and so must
search for God as an expression of our desire to be one
with him.

What means are most useful to me in recognizing
God's accessibility?

During those times when I do not sense God's presence and activity, what decisions do I make, what steps
do I take?

What characteristics of my life reflect my longing for
God and my desire to be united with him?

"Among Them
Were Women"

THE FOURTH SORROW

A great number of the people followed him, and among them were women who were beating their breasts and wailing for him. (Lk 23:27)

Though it is not explicitly articulated in the gospel stories of Jesus' Passion, Christian tradition has assumed that Mary remained as close to her son as permitted by the Roman procedures for a trial and the preparations for a crucifixion. If she was not able to accompany Jesus through the entirety of this journey, she surely would have encountered him at several points along the way from Herod's palace to Pilate's headquarters to Calvary. After all, this was designed to be a public spectacle. The people who followed Jesus on this death march were probably a diverse group, from the curious to the committed. The women mentioned in the above text were those who had cared for Jesus and the apostles, providing whatever resources were needed for the preaching missions. With Jesus arrested and the apostles dispersed, Mary was now in the company and care of these generous and faithful women.

After Jesus is sentenced by Pilate, the journey to Calvary begins. Lack of sleep, dehydration, and the tortures that preceded and prepared the prisoner for Roman crucifixion must have been clearly evident in Jesus as this parade of death made its way outside the city walls to the Place of the Skull. Though the direct distance between Pilate's fortress and the hill used for executions was not much more than one-fourth mile, given Jesus' treatment at the hands of the Jews and Romans, and his deteriorating physical condition over the previous few hours, any distance would feel much longer and more laborious. And for those who cared for him, the sight would be crushing. Yet they followed him, with Mary, accompanying him even on this journey.

The Sword

"The sword of the Lord devours from one end of the land to the other; no one shall be safe" (Jer 12:12). For those who understood something of Jesus' mission, for those who had seen and experienced the power of God at work through him, Jeremiah's words may express well their feelings at seeing Jesus condemned, beaten, and making his way up the hill to Calvary. This parade of death spared the prisoner no humiliation; anything could be heaped upon the parade's main attraction. Jeers and taunts from mock-makers, stones and dirt from fool-callers, beatings and curses from life-takers—every hostility and indignity could be cast on the condemned, anything was fair game. Family and friends were helpless, for no interference would be tolerated by those directing the parade. The deep recesses of Mary's heart are probed by the sword during the long moments of this journey.

The means by which the sword now unsheathes its honed edges are multifaceted. The betrayal by one of Jesus' close associates, the biased interrogation by the Hebrew elders, the hasty and politically weighted trial before Pilate, the executioners who push this parade forward—all these realities share in the creation of this spectacle and wield the sword that cuts so deeply. Yet this spectacle is the culmination of what Jesus had prepared for, practiced, and preached: complete obedience to God's will. Still, Mary's experience is marked by the pain that only a parent could know in these circumstances. Like all the others who knew Jesus and must watch him pass by, Mary is powerless to protect her son, preserve his dignity, or proclaim his innocence. But she can believe and love and hope.

After her role in the gospel infancy narratives by Saint Matthew and Saint Luke, Mary does not appear very much in the gospel stories. Saint John records her intervention at the wedding in Cana and recounts her standing at the foot of the cross, listening to Jesus in his dying moments. In Acts of the Apostles, Saint Luke notes her presence in the company of believers after the Resurrection and at Pentecost. Even though we may not have many details about Mary's life, it is evident that her journey leads toward the cross, and beyond. Our journey, too, will take similar pathways; encounters with the cross are inevitable in the spiritual life. Mary had to climb Calvary if she wanted to remain with Jesus. We should expect nothing different. The sword of distinction confronts us with the decision to remain near Jesus or to look for an alternate route. Mary's decision is clear.

The Challenge

"[The soldiers] led him away to crucify him" (Mt 27:31). Again Mary accompanies Jesus on a journey, this one from life to death. Unlike the trip to Egypt, Mary cannot protect Jesus now; she has no power to assure that he is far from those who would harm him. Nevertheless, she stays with him; where else would she be? Only on the surface does all this result from the petty machinations and political maneuvers between the Jewish leaders and the Roman authorities. If that were the only perspective to be considered, there would be no wisdom in exploring the deeper reality of God's activity on behalf of human salvation. Yet, grace is unfolding even as this journey progresses. There can be no uninvolved observers here; this journey must be accepted and chosen as the path to life even though only death looms on the horizon.

There will be dying to do on our way to union with God, if we choose to walk in the footsteps of Jesus. To think otherwise is to ignore—or at least refuse to acknowledge—the practical implications of the Paschal Mystery. If we are sincere in our efforts to be faithful in our relationship with God, consistent with whatever ensures and enriches our spiritual lives, and constant in our quest for Jesus, inevitably we will walk along the paths that lead to the cross. Fidelity, consistency, and constancy will have a definite impact on our lives; they will cost us something. The price is nothing less than accepting fully the death to self necessary so that we might be transformed in Jesus. If we are unwilling to pay that price, then our journey stalls, stagnates, and eventually stops altogether.

The challenge is to welcome and embrace that death to self, to deepen our union with God, serve others, and confirm our desire for eternal life. Our response to that challenge must be built on our identity by creation, the truth that we are made in God's image and likeness. Our response must also be based on our commitment as followers of Jesus, that we are privileged to share in the fullness of the Paschal Mystery. This identity and commitment indicate the direction in which our journey will advance. The quality of our response to the challenge will determine the caliber and the pace of our movement in that direction.

Dying to self is not a theoretical construct; it will have very real consequences in our everyday lives. First, it involves learning that there is much more to be considered than we can see and know within the narrow confines of our personal world, a world in which we have situated ourselves conveniently and conspicuously at the center. Christianity calls us to establish a different center around which our lives must revolve. Second, death to self entails understanding that our personal gifts and skills, and even our time, are resources to be used for the benefit of others. In fact, from the Christian perspective, this is their primary nature and purpose; if used solely for self, their value is undermined and their effectiveness is compromised.

The journey toward this death to self, toward the cross, strips us of all that is unnecessary for life. We can and usually do adopt many perspectives and priorities and practices that we assume are intrinsic to our identity and inseparable from our continued growth and development in the spiritual life. On this journey we gradually discover that the determinants for our identity and growth lie elsewhere, in God alone. The discovery urges us to reexamine the principles that guide our lives, to evaluate their lasting quality. Still, this journey can be unsettling and even frightening because it appears to empty us with no evident replenishment. Only with faith can we be assured that we are indeed advancing toward the very source of life.

Mary's Example

The fourth of Mary's sorrows unfolds on a journey, the *Via Dolorosa* itself, from the place of Jesus' trial to the Place of the Skull. It is not a long journey in terms of the distance to be traveled, but it is a journey that will reveal the deepest longings of the heart. Mary's example is without compromise. She had accompanied Jesus on other journeys during his life; now, as difficult and painful as this one would be, there can be no turning back or avoiding what lies ahead. "Whoever says 'I abide in him,' ought to walk just as he walked" (1 Jn 2:6). Mary has done precisely that.

Our spiritual lives advance by our acceptance of the journey opening before us. Acceptance does not include the assumption that the pathways of the journey will be pleasant always. Some may be, but we will definitely encounter dark and painful moments, times of confusion and uncertainty. This journey, then, is no casual and carefree stroll; it is a determined and decisive stride, always seeking to follow the directions that we believe God is calling us to pursue. Such a journey can advance only by our love for Jesus. The sword challenges us to courage and commitment. The sword awaits our response.

❧ For Reflection ❧

To be in Jesus' company always, Mary chose to follow him, regardless of where it would lead her. We, too, must make such a choice because the spiritual life is about following Jesus' example in the midst of our everyday lives. Because we choose to accompany Jesus and want to live his example, we will come to know the way of the cross.

In which situations am I most challenged to set aside my plans and expectations and simply follow Jesus, even though I do not know where it will lead?

How do I describe the spiritual growth I have experienced in such situations?

What kinds of events or experiences in my life have been and are the principal means through which Jesus calls me to accompany him?

"Standing Near the Cross of Jesus Was His Mother"

THE FIFTH SORROW

> Standing near the cross of Jesus were his mother, and his mother's sister, Mary the wife of Clopas, and Mary Magdalene. When Jesus saw his mother and the disciple whom he loved standing beside her, he said to his mother, "Woman, here is your son." Then he said to the disciple, "Here is your mother." And from that hour the disciple took her into his own home. (Jn 19:25–27)

Over the centuries, since that day on the hill outside Jerusalem, artists have depicted this scene in various ways. Sometimes it is presented with a starkness that reveals the grim reality of the situation; at other times the physical torments inflicted on the crucified are the specific focus; at yet other times a splendor emerges that highlights the glory of God's power and triumph over death. However this scene may be presented in art or literature, there is an inescapable truth here—this is a death-watch. For the family and friends of the one condemned to this humiliating death, life will not be the same. This person will no longer be with them; their lives will be altered and thus proceed down pathways for which they had not planned.

Though there are others present in this scene, what Jesus does here, he must accomplish alone. It is God's will. The death-watch is underway. Jesus' solitude becomes even more pronounced as he places his mother in the care of a beloved friend and disciple. In Saint John's Gospel, Jesus characterizes his approaching suffering and death in his prayer: "Father, the hour has come; glorify your Son so that the Son may glorify you" (17:1). The painful scene that now takes place on this hill of death is the moment of glorification. Mary is present of course. She is both a witness to and a participant in this work of salvation that Jesus is completing. For her, this is another encounter with the sword; and that sword cuts yet deeper as the life of her son flows away.

The Sword

Jesus' rapidly approaching death is the primary means by which the sword now strikes Mary's heart. However the intervening centuries may have buffered our awareness of all that was involved in Roman crucifixion, we still do know that this is a mother witnessing the brutal execution of her son. There are some other factors contributing to the depth with which Mary experienced this sword. First, this entire setting is compassionless. Though the biblical scholarship is not conclusive, it is likely that the hill on which Jesus died had been used as a place of execution for years and possibly for centuries. The place spoke only of death and the profound sadness of those who accompanied the condemned in their final hours. Second, Mary realized she would be alone after Jesus' death. Though there is no textual record of Joseph's death, tradition has assumed that Mary was a widow by the time of Jesus' execution. This sword is sharp indeed.

Yet we know that Mary is not left alone by the death of her son. With Jesus' words, Mary is placed in the care and companionship of his followers; she is among them as one of them. She is within that community of believers that Jesus gathers and forms into an apostolic force by his teaching, example, and the gift of the Holy Spirit. It is not evident through the gloom dominating this scene, but Mary becomes a part of the victory, the glorification that Jesus claims on the cross. She has a distinctive share in continuing the message and mission of Jesus within and through the company of his followers.

At this moment, though, Mary sees only her dying son. If there is any glory to be seen, only the eyes and heart of faith would provide the vision necessary to look beyond the horrors of this place and situation. We have the privilege of faith, the graced perspective of knowing that these events did lead to glory. Like Mary, we must take our place among the community of believers who live Jesus' example, proclaim his message, and continue his mission. We, too, will stand at the foot of the cross in our own lives. We can stand there in fear or in faith. Only in faith, though, will we come to know the power of the cross.

The Challenge

"Standing near the cross of Jesus was his mother." This statement is not at all surprising. Where else would Mary be at this point in Jesus' life? Though the setting is unquestionably in sharp contrast to her earlier experiences, once again she is at the temple. Her journey has brought her to this place where God is present. This temple holds the mystery of life for all to see or, more precisely, for all who by faith choose to see. Everything to which Mary had committed her life in response to God has guided her to this point. With fidelity and love she remains and stands firm. Where else would she be?

In our own spiritual lives we will come face to face with the cross. We cannot determine its specific timing or content, but encounters with the cross are inevitable if we are sincere in our desire and efforts to follow Jesus. During those encounters, our instincts may urge us to turn and run as if any other direction is the path to survival and life. The challenge is to remain faithful and stand firm so God's will can work within us. As the sword of distinction probes our heart during those encounters, it will reveal to us that Jesus is Savior, distinct from whatever other resources we may have relied upon for our salvation. Admittedly, because it is associated with the cross, that revelation will come with pain and darkness. With the eyes and heart of faith, however, we will be able to see the light and life that constitute the true nature of the cross.

In the cross we encounter the mystery of life, the presence of God. Though that mystery and presence will not be evident by the appearances and experiences associated with the cross, there is grace pulsating here; there is power in the weakness that the cross seems to represent and life in the death that it appears to bring. Faith sees beyond the apparent to the substantive so the power behind the weakness and the life beneath the death become discernible and desirable. Faith teaches us that turning away now would involve losing all that the spiritual life has meant thus far. We would try to seek life where there is no life and, thus, leave behind us the very source of life.

In the cross is the mystery of life. Apart from the graces that support us in our spiritual lives, we could neither accept nor even acknowledge the abundance of blessings offered to us through the cross. Faith enables us to accept that God is indeed at work in our encounters with the cross even though we do not see that work as it unfolds. Faith enables us to acknowledge that such encounters are expressions of God's love for us even though we do not experience that love by the standards to which we are accustomed. Such is the brilliance of God's grace—to work beyond what our capacities can see and accept, to love more than our senses can acknowledge and recognize. By faith we learn that the cross is a privilege.

In the cross is the gift of life. Sometimes we hear the expression that encounters with the cross can bring us to our knees. In truth, though, the cross brings us to our feet. We must stand, alert and attentive and accepting, if we are to embrace the full power of the cross. This gift of life is not easy, and we may not place it in the category of experiences we call pleasant, but this is the means to life that Jesus pioneered for us. This is the mystery into which our spiritual lives invite and initiate us. We must decide how we will respond to that invitation and if we will accept this initiation.

Mary's Example

The fifth of Mary's sorrows brings her to this place on a hill where humanity's salvation is accomplished through the death of her son. This place is truly a temple, for God is present. She stands, watches, listens, and even participates insofar as any mother suffers acutely at witnessing the death of her child. Mary's example demonstrates decision over despair, patience over passivity, strength over stoicism. While none of this made her experience any less painful, Mary knows that she must be present for her son and for herself. The letter to the Hebrews expresses well Mary's posture before the cross, and sets the standard for us. "Let us therefore approach the throne of grace with boldness, so that we may receive mercy and find grace in time of need" (4:16).

Our spiritual lives will thrive to the degree that we embrace the mystery of life, all of life, however and wherever it leads us. Inevitably there will be times when life gives us a share in the cross, and sometimes in large measure. We cannot control the nature of the crosses that come to us, but we can determine the caliber of our response to them. If we embrace those times decisively, patiently, and with faith and love and hope, then we will affirm that God is present and active even then, even now, always. The sword challenges us to welcome such a life. The sword awaits our response.

☞ For Reflection ☞

To remain faithful and stand firm, Mary stays with Jesus even when it is terribly painful for her, even when she is completely helpless to alter all that is taking place around her. Inevitably, we will encounter the cross. In that encounter, we have the freedom to run away or deny it or protest and complain. Or, we can remain and strive to discover what the cross teaches us about God's love for all humanity.

What crosses have I had to bear in life, and what crosses do I now bear?

How have and do those crosses shape my daily life and affect my spiritual growth?

What have I learned about Jesus through my encounters with the cross?

"PILATE GRANTED

THE BODY TO JOSEPH"

THE SIXTH SORROW

> When evening had come, and since it was
> the day of Preparation, that is, the day
> before the Sabbath, Joseph of Arimathea,
> a respected member of the council, who
> was also himself waiting expectantly for
> the kingdom of God, went boldly to
> Pilate and asked for the body of Jesus.
> Then Pilate wondered if he were already
> dead; and summoning the centurion, he
> asked him whether he had been dead for
> some time. When he learned from the
> centurion that he was dead, he granted the
> body to Joseph. (Mk 15:42–45)

After Jesus' death, his body was treated with more
decorum than was usually accorded to victims
of crucifixion. More often than not, the dead bodies
remained on the crosses and, eventually, were eaten away
by birds of prey and other animals that could reach them.
This practice was both a visible deterrent for others who
might seek to undermine the supremacy of Roman rule,
and a further indignity heaped upon the deceased and
the family. Jesus' case is considered an exception because

a request is made in light of the solemn Sabbath that was approaching. Pilate's permission is required and a Jewish official, an elder, makes the request. Once this request was granted, the scene of Mary receiving the body of Jesus can unfold.

After confirming that Jesus was dead, Pilate may have acceded to this request for several reasons. There had been controversy surrounding the arrest, trial, and sentencing of Jesus. Granting this request could placate Jewish sensitivities regarding the presence of dead bodies on public display during religious feasts, thus making this whole episode more quickly forgotten. And the person making the request is a respected dignitary in the Jewish community; it would have been in Pilate's best interests to make this gesture of generosity. Mary must wait while all the necessary political machinations are accomplished. Finally, all is done, and Joseph of Arimathea removes the body.

The Sword

The body of the son that is now returned to the mother has little if any resemblance to the one she knew so well and cared for so often as he was growing up. As Mary held Jesus in life, she now holds him in death; these two are finally reunited after the fatal events of this day. There is no reason to assume that Mary would have departed the

scene of the crucifixion before Jesus' death; tradition thus
assumes that she was present at and probably participated
in the pre-burial prayers and rituals. The somber reunion
prior to burial, in reality, did not reflect the majestic and
contemplative image of Michelangelo's *Pieta*. Everything
had to be done as quickly as possible because of the
approaching Sabbath; everyone had to get home in time
for the beginning of the religious feast. Holding her son,
Mary once again feels the power and penetration of the
sword.

The means through which the sword now strikes is
Joseph of Arimathea. He is a "good and righteous man"
(Lk 23:50), a man of hope who was "waiting expectantly
for the kingdom of God" (Mk 15:43), and "a disciple of
Jesus, though a secret one because of his fear of the Jews"
(Jn 19:38). He managed to accomplish all that was necessary for Mary to receive the body of Jesus. Mary's sense of
loss, pain, and loneliness here can be understood by mil-
lions of parents over the centuries and even now who have
borne the horror and helplessness of holding their son or
daughter who has died. That experience is only intensified
if the parent has witnessed the death as Mary did.

This scene beneath the cross, at the place of execution,
could appear to be the final one in this story; we might
assume all is done. But another journey is opening, a
journey of faith. Mary must believe that there is yet more
to her life with Jesus because of God's promises to her so

many years before. And God is faithful. Mary's faith and love even at this moment may have empowered her to pray once again those words from another, though less painful, time of confusion and wonderment. "My soul magnifies the Lord, and my spirit rejoices in God my Savior . . . for the Mighty One has done great things for me, and holy is his name" (Lk 1:46–47, 49). Now especially, for this journey, Mary needed to believe that God "has looked with favor on the lowliness of his servant" (Lk 1:48).

The Challenge

This is a journey in faith. It brings us to moments of convergence between hope and despair, certainty and ignorance, light and darkness, life and death. We journey with a Jesus that we no longer recognize on the basis of our earlier experiences. This Jesus is betrayed, beaten, and broken. This Jesus does not reflect the image that we expect from someone who is the very source of comfort and consolation. This Jesus seems foreign to everything we have known and assumed about him to this point in our spiritual life. The sword of distinction bids us to remain united to Jesus by love, even when we do not recognize or understand his presence and activity. We will be able to see him, but only with the eyes of faith, only with eyes capable and willing to look beyond our expectations and assumptions.

This journey in faith acknowledges that the death of Jesus must be a part of our own spiritual life. We make this journey with the death of Jesus so that we might assimilate it into our lives and be transformed by it. The mystery of life inherent in the cross beckons us to embrace fully the example of Jesus. Our encounter with the cross and this death are substantive components of our journey toward union with God and fullness of life. This is the pattern established by Jesus, and Mary is the pioneer in that journey. This cross and death probe deeply, revealing corners and crevices of our lives that we might prefer not to see. But to bypass this experience would be to turn away from the transformative power of Jesus' example.

We must trust and pray; that is the challenge. The alternative is to rely on our own resources and so compromise the direction that our spiritual lives have taken thus far in response to grace. Our trust must be grounded in the constant and consistent work of God's grace and the truth of God's promises. Our prayer must be sustained by a faithfulness that knows the power of that grace and the greatness of those promises. Trust and prayer may not be particularly weighty challenges when our experiences in the spiritual life resonate with evidence of God's presence and activity. We may begin to think that our spiritual life could not be otherwise.

But other experiences do emerge, times when it may not be so easy to celebrate God's care and concern precisely because we sense nothing of them. What about those times when there are no signs of life around us? What about the periods when all we seem to hold is darkness and death? Then the challenge to trust and pray is before us, in all its starkness, awaiting our response. When we are questioning and wondering about the direction of our spiritual lives and the veracity of what has transpired, it is then that we must trust the new life that can emerge from death, and pray with the fidelity that nurtures patience and perspective.

This journey in faith, this journey with the death of Jesus, is an essential aspect of our spiritual lives. It is necessary for the transformation that must take place within us. It challenges us to rely on God alone, even during those times when we have no evidence of God's proximity to us or involvement with us. At such times it is only by faith that we can embrace the truth of God's closeness to us, only by faith that we can acknowledge and accept that this journey will lead to life. Like Mary, we too must believe that God has done and is doing great things for us. And, whatever our experience may be, the truth stands firm— holy is God's name.

Mary's Example

The sixth of Mary's sorrows is stark. What we see here is yet part of the journey and, depending upon our perspective, it can be viewed as a moment of despair, of abandonment, or a moment of tender love. Mary's example affirms the need to embrace Jesus however and whenever he comes to be united with us. Like her, we too must accept and love even in such painful circumstances. Our journey will be marked by that embrace, acceptance, and love precisely because in our bodies we carry "the death of Jesus, so the life of Jesus may also be made visible in our bodies" (2 Cor 4:10).

Our spiritual lives will be shaped by the cross. We must come to peace with the truth that the cross can never be relegated to the realm of being merely possible or even probable. It is inevitable precisely because it is the pattern established by Jesus. Our willingness to accept and love the crucified Jesus, as did Mary, leads us ever deeper into the mystery of life inherent in the cross. The sword challenges us to embrace this death so we can continue our journey toward another life, a new and eternal life. The sword awaits our response.

✎ For Reflection ✎

To be focused on God, to be a realist in responding to all that had transpired, Mary had to accept the cross and death of her son as part of God's love and plan for her life. The crosses we encounter reflect God's work and love even though nothing of those may be evident in what we are experiencing. Usually, we recognize God's work and love only with the grace of hindsight; time can sharpen our perspective and clarify our understanding.

Which crosses in my past do I now recognize as expressions of God's love for me?

How does that recognition influence the approach I want to take in responding to future encounters with the cross?

What personal gifts or qualities do I see in my life that flow from having experienced and accepted a particular cross?

"THEY LAID
JESUS THERE"

THE SEVENTH SORROW

> They took the body of Jesus and wrapped
> it with the spices in linen cloths, accord-
> ing to the burial custom of the Jews. Now
> there was a garden in the place where he
> was crucified, and in the garden was a new
> tomb in which no one had ever been laid.
> And so, because it was the Jewish day of
> Preparation, and the tomb was nearby,
> they laid Jesus there. (Jn 19:40–42)

This brief and hurried scene followed very shortly after
Pilate's permission had been granted and Jesus' body
was removed from the cross. Saint Luke's Gospel specifies
that "the women who had come with him from Galilee
followed, and they saw the tomb and how his body was
laid" (23:55). Since Mary had accompanied Jesus to the
summit of this hill of death, it is assumed that she was
part of the burial rites for her son, at least as an attentive observer. Having completed this ritual and knowing
that the restrictions of the Sabbath were pressing closer
with each passing moment, everyone now returns home.
Though Saint John's Gospel combines the anointing and
burial of Jesus, Saints Mark and Luke record that the

women return to the tomb after the Sabbath to perform the anointings and prayers associated with Jewish burial (cf. Mk 16:1; Lk 23:56–24:1).

Whatever the precise sequence of events after Jesus' death, for Mary the stark reality is that even the body is gone from sight now. The immediacy of her physical connection with Jesus has been brutally severed. The tomb is sealed, and Mary goes home. The quiet and rest of the coming Sabbath would be in sharp contrast to the noise and rush—and horror—of the past few hours. Solitude and silence now surround Mary. Though such qualities are usually refreshing, in this instance they may have highlighted the awful reality of Jesus' absence. With the psalmist, Mary could pray, "God, you have put me in the depths of the Pit, in the regions dark and deep" (Ps 88:6). The sword now pierces most deeply, even to those places in the heart where only hope can provide light.

The Sword

The final strike of the sword is particularly poignant for Mary. She witnesses the closing of the tomb and experiences the void of Jesus' absence. It is a void that cannot be filled. As the crowd disappears, the noise goes with them and any commotion that could serve as a distraction from the awful stillness and silence of this death. It is finished. Mary's journey has brought her to this point, alone and childless, even as she was those many years ago at the Annunciation. And yet, her life is so much more than a mere recycling of familiar places and experiences. It has been a spiral of intensifying sorrows, stripping her of what is most precious. Even the realization that this is God's work and will does not lessen the pain and finality of her loss.

In raising Jesus and relating to him during the years leading up to this day on Calvary, Mary no doubt was challenged to embrace that detachment which finds its meaning in faith and hope. Surviving this strike of the sword demands nothing less. She must ground herself in a fidelity that is rooted in her love for God and her commitment to Jesus. While those qualities do not dull the sword's sharp edges, they do affirm her integrity in living the truth of what she said many years before: "Here am I, the servant of the Lord; let it be with me according to your word" (Lk 1:38).

Jesus had predicted the Passion; the disciples and others had heard his gruesome description of how he would be betrayed by one of his own and then mistreated by the leaders of the people. Mary, too, must have heard or been told what Jesus had said. Even though his followers had that information, it does not displace the shock and emptiness experienced now that he is dead and buried. The pain must be borne. Jesus had also promised the resurrection; the disciples had heard him speak of this, though it struck them as incomprehensible. Misinterpretation of what he meant could run rampant and even be used against them. Now that the tomb was closed and sealed, faith alone would be the guide for the days ahead. "Faith is the assurance of things hoped for, the conviction of things not seen" (Heb 11:1). Such faith they would take with them, in fear for the future, behind closed doors. Such faith would be necessary if they were to face the power of the sword.

The Challenge

Having completed the rituals for burial, the small group that accompanied Jesus' body to the tomb now gather the aftereffects of the day's events, in their hands and in their hearts. It is time to depart this place. After the final words of commendation are prayed over the body, the group moves outside so the tomb can be sealed. There is nothing more to say or do. Mary is enveloped by silence and separation as she departs with the group. The horrors of this day have stilled their voices and drained their emotions; yet there is longing in their hearts as they return to their homes.

In this intense experience of separation from God, the temple and the journey converge. The challenge for us at such times is to embrace the wisdom of the temple in faith and the blessing of the journey in hope. No academic or scientific certainty can satisfy the heart's longing. Temple wisdom and journey blessing are means to union with God. We will not always see and sense that we are actually moving toward such union. In fact, such sight and sense can be rare even though the desire for such union is strong and stable. Only faith can provide the eyes to see; only hope can enable the heart to sense.

Apart from this faith and hope, our growth and development in the spiritual life would lack forward movement, going in a circle without any real progress. Any genuine movement would be constantly hindered or completely halted. We can hinder or halt our spiritual lives whenever we choose to advance—or attempt to—by relying solely on our own methods, depending only on our own efforts, to sustain us. However skilled our methods or sophisticated our efforts, inevitably we will be frustrated by the realization that our exertions are insufficient.

Saint Paul articulates the principal pathways for the spiritual life. First, "we walk by faith, not by sight" (2 Cor 5:7). We must remain faithful without the benefit of all the clear indicators we would like to set up as guideposts along the way. Second, "hope that is seen is not hope. Who hopes for what is seen? But if we hope for what we do not see, then we wait for it with patience" (Rom 8:24–25). We must trust and be willing to continue on our way without knowing what may yet unfold before us. Third, "the greatest of these is love" (1 Cor 13:13). Only by love can we reflect the living likeness of Jesus. Faith and hope and love are the lights we need to face and move beyond the tomb.

By our usual standards and expectations, death and separation from God appear to have little to do with the markers along the pathways to eternal life and union with God. Faith, hope, and love teach us otherwise; we are challenged to accept that God is present with us, guiding us, and ever caring for us. Whatever our immediate experiences may lead us to think, the meaning and mission and mystery of our lives are linked intimately to God. Only in faith, hope, and love can we stand before an experience of God that reflects the tomb and not despair. Only with faith, hope, and love is it possible to accept that such an experience is not an ending to life but truly a beginning.

Mary's Example

This last of Mary's sorrows leads her to silence and separation. All that she has experienced in the temple and on the journey meet here at this tomb that holds her son. Mary's example is a witness of her conviction that God remains faithful. She lives and knows the truth of Ezekiel's prophecy, "you shall know that it was not without cause that I did all that I have done, says the Lord God" (Ez 14:23). Even in the darkest moments, Mary's life has proclaimed her fidelity to God; thus, "from now on all generations will call me blessed" (Lk 1:48). And so it has come to pass in our days.

In our spiritual lives, we may have to travel pathways similar to Mary's own, pathways that bring us to darkness and sorrow and pain. But these pathways teach us that death and separation, however they appear in our experience, are but the preludes to new life. The sharp and scrutinizing sword of distinction will probe our heart, but only to strengthen us that we might advance without stumbling on circumstances and encounters that could disappoint, dismay, or discourage us. This sword detaches us from everything so we can learn to live by faith, love, and hope. The sword challenges us to embrace this teaching that we might be free of whatever would hinder our way. The sword awaits our response.

For Reflection

To trust in all God's promises to her, to believe the teachings of her son, Mary had to hope even when nothing around her provided a cause for hope. We are called to trust and believe that God is part of our lives, though our observation and experience tell us otherwise. Such is the ground for the hope that supplies energy and direction for our lives.

What supports my hope that God is at work in my life and world, and how do I maintain those supports?

What barriers to hope do I encounter, and how can I overcome those barriers?

Are there ways in which I have recognized and can recognize the cross as a sign of hope?

MARY OF SORROWS

TEACHER AND EXAMPLE

As evident in Mary's story, the temple is not merely a physical place. It is the experience of being set apart, realigning one's focus, to listen for God's words and learn God's ways. The origin of the word temple reflects this; it refers to dividing and separating, not to destroy but to dedicate, to recognize the sacredness of the present moment. In the temple we listen for God's words and watch for God's ways. Similarly, the journey is not simply the movement from one location to another; that would be better described as travel. The journey is a time of transition, a passage in life that can alter our perspectives and even our priorities because of the insight and knowledge that we acquire along the way. Unlike travel, the caliber of the journey cannot be measured by distance and time. It can be gauged only by the quality of our lives. On the journey we live God's words and ways.

This is the dynamic within Mary's experience of and response to the seven events that have been explored in these reflections. Her example can be a model for our own spiritual lives. Our lives will be marked by the temple and journey, even though our experiences will not necessarily parallel Mary's own. We have and will continue to encounter events and circumstances that set us apart and challenge us to realign our priorities that we might fix our attention on God's presence and activity. We have and will continue to know times and moments that change our lives and challenge us to move beyond our usual routine that we might respond to God without hesitation or procrastination. The temple and the journey can transform us. Mary of Sorrows is a wise teacher and a sure example as the grace of that transformation works within us.

LEARNING FROM MARY OF SORROWS

We can learn from Mary's experiences even though they are uniquely her own. Her response, participation, and cooperation reflect some essential attitudes for the spiritual life. If we are open to learn from her example, then we can nurture our capacity and willingness to respond to, participate in, and cooperate with God's presence and activity in our lives. What attitudes does Mary of Sorrows teach us in these seven moments of her life?

Listening

Thus the spiritual life begins. Though Mary may have attended the temple presentation of other children among her relatives or friends, this one is particularly special for her. It is now her son being presented, her son being offered to God. She listens to the ritual prayers of blessing, attentive to whatever may be spoken about him. What she hears in that listening is an ominous prophecy about his destiny and about her future. Mary is in the temple.

We, too, are called to listen. God's word can be spoken to us in so many ways. If we are not attentive, it is altogether possible to miss what is said either by distraction or because it is drowned by the noise—internal and external—that regularly bombards us and conspires to dominate our attention. God's instruction to us through the psalmist is most wise, "Be still, and know that I am God" (Ps 46:10). We can listen in the stillness, and hear. In the listening, we come to know God, and so our spiritual lives continue.

Safeguarding

The spiritual life carries no guarantees that it will be easy or proceed smoothly. More than likely, Mary would never have expected an urgent trip to a foreign land with her young child and husband. Nor could she have predicted that the whims of an insecure king would make such a trip imperative. It is a time for extraordinary measures, a time for protecting her son even more than her natural, maternal instinct typically required. Life and family are the priorities here. Familiar and cherished friends, neighbors, and surroundings must be left behind to safeguard those priorities. Mary takes up the journey.

Whatever our expectations and however extensive our precautions to assure the progress of our spiritual lives, difficult, challenging, and unanticipated moments will emerge. While we must be vigilant in the face of such moments and when confronting the many realities that could erode the spiritual life, we should not thereby encase it in cement as insurance that nothing will change. Rather than serving as a safeguard, such an encasement becomes a sepulcher. We must be willing to move beyond the familiar and the comfortable whenever necessary to protect and nurture our relationship with God. That protection and nurturance are neither self-generating nor self-sustaining; we must take responsibility for them. "So acknowledge today and take to heart that the Lord is God in heaven above and on the earth beneath; there is no other." (Dt 4:39). We must be willing to enter the journey with that acknowledgment and go wherever it leads us.

Searching

The spiritual life will be marked by times that speak to us only of loss. A parent's nightmare: losing a child. What might begin as a simple feeling of not knowing where the wanderings of a curious child have led quickly becomes an intense panic when the realization hits that the child is not just around the nearest corner or in some favorite hiding place. Mary and Joseph retrace their steps and search for their son. The search is extensive, time-consuming, and exhausting. Finally, a reunion of parents and child does occur, but it has peculiar qualities. Jesus speaks of his emerging mission; Mary ponders what all this means, now and for the future. She is in the temple.

The spiritual life is work and takes time precisely because it is a living reality. In our relationship with God, as in any relationship we value, there will be moments of closeness and separation, fullness and emptiness, growth and dryness. We search for God during those times of separation and emptiness and dryness, not to compensate for any negligence on our part, though negligence is always a possibility. We search because we long to be with God, we desire to maintain and strengthen that relationship. We search because we love God. We search because we believe that God is accessible, even if our experience tells us otherwise. With this belief, we trust that God is close to us. With this belief, we can recognize that what

God calls us to do "is something very near to us, already in our mouths and in our hearts; we have only to carry it out" (Dt 30:14).

The Learning

These three moments of Mary's experience reflect those dimensions of the spiritual life that are traditionally referred to as active. Though grace is always at work throughout our spiritual journey, these dimensions require our efforts and discipline for maintaining the health and progress of our relationship with God. The spiritual life is an invitation. We must listen for God's call to us, safeguard whatever will assist us in responding to that call, and search for the means and ways that will bring us ever closer to him. The active dimensions demonstrate that the spiritual life is not self-propelled, and we are not merely passengers; we must use the graces we are given and the abilities we have developed to assure continuity and consistency in our response to God. These dimensions remind us of Saint Paul's instruction to "work out your own salvation with fear and trembling; for it is God who is at work in you, enabling you both to will and to work for his good pleasure" (Phil 2:12–13).

The example of Mary of Sorrows gives us some insight regarding this challenge of working out our salvation, of willing and working for God's pleasure. In these first three instances, Jesus is yet a child, vulnerable. Mary must be especially attentive and watchful regarding the security and quality of his life. That same attentiveness and watchfulness must mark our attitude and approach to our practice of the spiritual life. The alternative is clear; the value and priority we assign to our spiritual lives would gradually diminish and eventually disappear.

Listening, safeguarding, and searching, as the active dimensions of our spiritual lives, cannot be characterized as merely sequential and chronological. They do not strictly follow one another over a specified period of time after which we move on without ever needing to address them again. Much more do they constitute a continuing dynamic that facilitates the progress of our movement toward union with God. As God's word is spoken to us, we listen. When distracted from the responsibilities of responding to that word, we safeguard our focus and redirect our attention. If areas of our lives distance us from God's word and dull our sensitivity to it, then we search for and take those pathways that will lead us in the direction where he awaits us. This is what Mary of Sorrows teaches us, this is what we must learn.

LIVING WITH MARY OF SORROWS

The attitudes that we learn from Mary's example must be lived if we truly want them to have any real meaning for us. They cannot be mere fashion accessories; they must be decisions that shape the quality of our lives. Such decisions, however, are not solely our own invention, they are in response to God's grace. Even more, they invite God to work within us, and they express our commitment to cooperate with that work. Mary of Sorrows sets a pattern of life before us. What are we called to live?

Accompanying

The spiritual life is not for those who would prefer to be spectators; it requires a commitment. Mary remains as close to Jesus as the procedures for Roman executions will allow. She is no mere spectator on this painful journey from the praetorium in the city to the pinnacle of Calvary. For her, as for her son, this is the time for accomplishing all that God has asked; this is the time for allowing God's will to unfold regardless of what it may bring. There can be no turning back. For Mary, though this experience is painful, as it would be for any mother, love for her son and obedience to God assure the choice she has made. Her integrity and sincerity and fidelity are evidence of her decision to accompany her son even now.

Our spiritual lives must involve more than contenting ourselves to be carried along by current trends and rapidly developing events. We must take a decisive stance by which we choose to follow and remain close to Jesus regardless of where that might lead us. Neither the timing nor the destination of our spiritual lives will be under our control. If we choose to be companions of Jesus, then we embrace where he goes because we want to live the fullness of his words, "You did not choose me but I chose you" (Jn 15:16). We choose to be faithful to him and to follow the pathways in which he leads us precisely because we have been chosen.

The dynamic of choosing to follow the Lord Jesus because we have been chosen reflects a transitional period in the spiritual life that can be set apart from both the preceding and the following moments. It is a time when God assumes a more active and direct role and thus our posture is to welcome and accept what he is doing. We are willing companions. Such a transition is especially challenging because, as our spiritual lives progress, we will become accustomed to our routines and patterns. We will be comfortable with having a determinative influence on and even control over the pace and practice of our spiritual lives. This transitional time brings us to a point at which we recognize our diminishing influence and control and thus experience that a hand and a heart other than our own are guiding the directions we take and the decisions we make. This is a transformative period during which God's will and ways within us are gradually transfiguring our will and ways into the likeness of Jesus' own.

Remaining

Encounters with the cross are inevitable in our spiritual lives. Whatever stories Mary may have heard about Roman crucifixion, however graphic the images she may have conjured, all this would have been overpowered by the realities she witnessed on Calvary that day. As part of the crowd, there were times during that day when she was physically close to Jesus. Nevertheless, she could not reach out, hold, and protect him as she had done when he was a child. There were no words or gestures with sufficient maternal force to make this situation better. This is God's will. Her son must now complete his mission—alone—by doing all that God has asked. Mary remains near; she can do little else other than love her son as she had always done.

The cross, however it is manifested in our lives, is not supplemental to the spiritual life; it is substantive to our progress toward union with God. It is part of the example established for us by Jesus. Whether or not we recognize or acknowledge it as such when and how it emerges in our lives, the cross is a sacred moment; it is evidence of God's transforming work underway within us. Our experience of the cross, more than likely, will not match our expectations and anticipations of what such a transformation could or should involve. We may be tempted—and sometimes urged by others—to turn away and try to reinstate some former time so the reality of the cross will not be so stark for us. All such efforts, ultimately, deceive us, deny what is before us, and delay the work of grace in us. Mary's example challenges us to remain, to trust that the cross can and will be life-giving for us, even as new life followed Jesus' death. "Trust in the Lord with all your heart, and do not rely on your own insight" (Prv 3:5).

Accepting

That the course of events unfolding around us cannot be altered will be evident at times. Then we must accept that truth, however unclear or unpleasant it may be. Mary again holds Jesus even as she did so many times when he was but a child. Now, however, she receives from him no gesture of recognition, no joyful smile from son to mother, in fact, no sign of life. Nothing she could do would change all that has transpired, however profound her instincts may be to do so. These events have changed her life radically; her son is dead. It is as if she has journeyed to another plane of existence, so devoid of life were her surroundings on that hill outside the city.

Periods of absence, darkness, and even a sense of otherworldliness can mark the pathways of our spiritual lives. We may experience a loss of meaning and direction, and we can be paralyzed by the uncertainty that accompanies not knowing which way to go or what to do. We may want to fill the emptiness and light the darkness by reclaiming perspectives and practices that are comfortable and familiar to us. The challenge is to accept what is before us as yet another facet of God's presence and activity. Such acceptance is not defeatist; it reflects Mary's response at the Annunciation and Jesus' response in Gethsemane. Our response, also, must be nothing less than accepting the priority of God's will and way over our own. However difficult, painful, or confusing the situation or experience may be, we can turn to Job for a reminder of the challenge before us. "The Lord gave, and the Lord has taken away; blessed be the name of the Lord. . . . Shall we receive good at the hand of God, and not receive the bad?" (Jb 1:21; 2:10).

Hoping

There will be times in our spiritual lives when all that remains is hope; it will be all we can hold onto in the face of the emptiness and dryness we experience. Mary has stayed with Jesus throughout the painful events preceding and during his execution. She held him in life, then in death, and now she must offer him to God even as she first offered him before Simeon when this story began. By experience she now knows the temple and the journey. It is a sacred moment, a time set apart, as she commends her son's body to the tomb. It is also a moment of transition, of change, as she turns and walks into the future not knowing what it may hold. Still, she can hope.

In our spiritual lives, experiences of distance from God and darkness covering our awareness of God hold the potential to lead us to discouragement and even despair. Only hope will provide the compass settings we need to continue on our way. Hope is not magic; it will not take away our experiences. But it can root us in the conviction that God continues to be a part of our lives even when we do not perceive his presence. In trust, based on that conviction, we can pray with the psalmist, "For God alone my soul waits in silence, for my hope is from him. God alone is my rock and my salvation, my fortress; I shall not be shaken. On God rests my deliverance and my honor; my mighty rock, my refuge is in God" (Ps 62:5–7).

The Living

These last four moments of Mary's experience reflect those dimensions of the spiritual life that are traditionally referred to as passive. As grace continues its transforming work within us, God guides our spiritual lives more directly and surely than our own efforts are capable of doing. The spiritual life requires patience and passion, born of our desire to accompany the Lord, to be with the Lord, along whatever pathways God's will may lead us. We must remain steadfast regardless of what we encounter, accept the ways of God's grace within us, and hope confidently in God's presence with us and promise to us. The passive dimensions remind us that our spiritual lives are, ultimately, God's work; we must cooperate with that work, asking God to remove from us whatever could delay or disrupt the completion of that work. These dimensions call us to acknowledge, with the prophet Isaiah, "Lord, you will ordain peace for us, for indeed, all that we have done, you have done for us" (Is 26:12).

The example of Mary of Sorrows reflects this truth from Isaiah. Before these final scenes, Jesus had made statements and decisions that led him to the Passion. Mary could neither control nor alter the events she had witnessed, as painful as they were for her. She chooses to remain as close to Jesus as possible and permissible; she has remained and is now faithful, recognizing that God's will must be done. This was her response to the angel many years before, and so it is even now; indeed, that response has marked her entire life. And so it must be for us.

Remaining, accepting, and hoping, as the passive dimensions of our spiritual lives, in no way diminish the responsibility we have of cooperating with God. During periods when we experience that our spiritual lives do not appear to be advancing because it is no longer completely under our control, we must be faithful and responsive to God's ways. Such fidelity and response, though necessary for continued growth, cannot assure that we will understand those ways. We may prefer to take up some former practices that will provide us with a recognizable measure that indicates that we are moving. However strong that preference, we must be patient, faithful, and confident that grace is at work, that God's will is unfolding within us. This is what Mary of Sorrows demonstrates for us; this is what we must live.

THE WOMAN
AND THE SWORD:

Companion and Guide

Mary of Sorrows is a wise companion and an experienced guide as we travel the pathways of the spiritual life. We can rely confidently on her wisdom and experience as we make our way toward union with God. Mary's encounters with the temple and the journey are steady and sure; they provide us with instruction and insight into those graces that animate, advance, and amplify our spiritual lives.

The spiritual life is animated by God's grace; however, that grace does not work in complete isolation from our efforts and commitment. If it did, we would be little more than bystanders in our own spiritual lives. As it is, though, our willing efforts to root our identity in God alone and our wholehearted commitment to continued development are essential elements in the spiritual life. We bear the responsibility of demonstrating our seriousness about the spiritual life and our sincerity in cooperating with God's work.

The spiritual life advances through God's grace; however, that grace is not alien to the specifics of our daily lives. If it were, we would recognize nothing of the invitation and incentive that God regularly extends to us. As it is, our quest for union with God through daily life and our acceptance of the death to self that accompanies such a quest are necessary components of the spiritual life. God's presence and activity are given flesh within that quest and acceptance. The progress of our spiritual lives can be compromised by complacency in responding to the grace that God makes available to us.

The spiritual life is amplified with God's grace; however, that grace will not force us to grow in ways we resist and in areas we refuse to explore. If it did, we would have no responsibility for our spiritual development. As it is, our fidelity to all means of growth and our trust that God remains faithful are inseparable from the expanding horizons our spiritual lives strive to incorporate. God is faithful, God is loving; fidelity and trust must be our response to that faithfulness and love. These are basic factors characteristic of any lasting growth in the spiritual life.

Mary of Sorrows demonstrates that we must fully embrace every dimension of our spiritual lives if we truly want to respond to God's grace, if we desire union with God, and if we seek a share in all that the life and teaching of Jesus promise us. Mary of Sorrows will accompany and guide us as the pathways of the spiritual life bring us to encounters with the temple and the journey. Our experiences ever remain distinct from hers, but we too must welcome the works and the ways of God's grace in our lives. We, too, will meet the death that heralds the resurrection.

"I will hope in God"

The woman and the sword. The woman has remained faithful even as the sword has struck ever deeper. Mary of Sorrows is usually depicted with seven swords piercing her heart, recalling these difficult events in her life. Still, there is but one sword passing through all these events, the sword of distinction that probed and affirmed Mary's faith, love, and hope. This is the sword of transformation that unites her with Jesus for all generations even as it united her to him during those events.

Jesus is revealed as prophet in the temple of Jerusalem and as savior on the temple of the cross. At the presentation and the crucifixion, Mary's faith is deepened by the piercing of the sword. Jesus is enfolded in Mary's arms on the journey to Egypt to preserve life, and after being lowered to her from his death on the cross. United to Jesus through life and death, Mary's love is perfected in the power of the sword. For three days, Jesus is separated from Mary on the trip from Jerusalem and by the tomb in the garden. Through this uncertainty and loneliness, Mary's hope is confirmed with the penetration of the sword. Jesus' journey places him on the way to Calvary; so too does Mary's journey place her, and so will our journey place us.

The woman and the sword. This woman of faith stands always by the Lord. This woman of love is one with the Lord in all things. This woman of hope desires only the Lord. Mary of Sorrows is this woman, distinguished and transformed by the sword for all to see, for all times. Mary of Nazareth can proclaim these prophetic words, for truly she has lived them. "I am one who has seen affliction. . . . God has driven and brought me into darkness without any light. . . . But this I call to mind, and therefore I have hope: the steadfast love of the Lord never ceases, his mercies never come to an end; they are new every morning; great is your faithfulness. 'The Lord is my portion,' says my soul, 'therefore I will hope in him'" (Lam 3:1, 2, 21–24). So it has been for her. So it must be for us.

STABAT MATER

The liturgical hymn most frequently associated with Our Lady of Sorrows is the *Stabat Mater Dolorosa*. Its title is simply the first three words of the Latin hymn and refers to Mary on Calvary standing at the foot of Jesus' cross. The text of the hymn highlights the union of Mary and all Christians with the suffering and death of Jesus. Though it focuses on the anguish that Mary experienced at the death of her son, the hymn does point to the transformation and new life that are the blessings of union with Christ crucified. The *Stabat Mater* celebrates Mary's faithful presence on Calvary and invites us to that same fidelity in our daily lives.

The precise origins of the hymn are lost to history. Its authorship has been ascribed to a range of people and popes from the early seventh century to the late fourteenth century, including Saints Gregory the Great, Bernard of Clairvaux, and Bonaventure. It was widely known by the end of the fourteenth century, used in various religious services and processions during the following centuries, and formally included in the Roman Missal by Pope Benedict XIII in 1727. At that time the commemoration of the Seven Dolors of the Blessed Virgin Mary was celebrated on the Friday after Passion Sunday.

Over the centuries, the *Stabat* drew the attention and interest of musical composers. Liturgical ceremonies were often important and convenient venues for familiarizing large audiences with their work even while contributing to the solemnity of church services. Composers used the text to create elaborate settings for chorus and orchestra. A sampling of those who composed music for the *Stabat* include Giovanni Pierluigi da Palestrina, Agostino Seffani, Alessandro Scarlatti, Giovanni Battista Pergolesi, Luigi Boccherini, Joseph Haydn, Giuseppe Verdi, Gioachino Rossini, Franz Shubert, and Antonín Dvorák.

What follows are two translations. The first, a traditional translation, is taken from the Catholic Roman Missal and is used as the Sequence or Chant before the Gospel Alleluia on September 15, the feast of Our Lady of Sorrows. The second, a contemporary translation, is one among several anonymous texts that can be found in various publications and on the internet. The many ways in which this hymn has been preserved and presented through the centuries are a testimony to its enduring value.

Traditional Translation

At the cross her station keeping,
stood the mournful Mother weeping,
close to Jesus to the last.
Through her heart, his sorrow sharing,
all his bitter anguish bearing,
now at length the sword had passed!

Oh, how sad and sore distressed,
was that Mother highly blessed
of the sole-begotten One!
Christ above in torment hangs,
she beneath beholds the pangs
of her dying, glorious Son.

Is there one who would not weep,
'whelmed in miseries so deep,
Christ's dear mother to behold?
Can the human heart refrain
from partaking in her pain,
in that mother's pain untold?

Bruised, derided, cursed, defiled,
she beheld her tender child,
all with bloody scourges rent.
For the sins of his own nation
saw him hang in desolation
till his spirit forth he sent.

O sweet Mother! Font of love,
touch my spirit from above,
make my heart with yours accord.
Make me feel as you have felt;
make my soul to glow and melt
with the love of Christ, my Lord.

Holy Mother, pierce me through,
in my heart each wound renew
of my Savior crucified.
Let me share with you his pain,
who for all our sins was slain,
who for me in torments died.

Let me mingle tears with you,
mourning him who mourned for me,
all the days that I may live.
By the cross with you to stay,

there with you to weep and pray,
is all I ask of you to give.

Virgin of all virgins blest!
Listen to my fond request:
let me share your grief divine.
Let me to my latest breath,
in my body bear the death
of that dying son of yours.

Wounded with his every wound,
steep my soul till it has swooned
in his very Blood away.
Be to me, O Virgin, nigh,
lest in flames I burn and die,
in his awful judgment day.

Christ, when you shall call me hence,
be your Mother my defense,
by your cross my victory.
While my body here decays,
may my soul your goodness praise,
safe in heaven eternally. Amen.

Contemporary Translation

The grieving Mother stood weeping beside the cross where her Son was hanging;

her weeping soul, compassionate and grieving, was pierced by the sword.

How sad and afflicted was that blessed Mother of the sole-begotten One

who mourned and grieved and trembled looking at the torment of her glorious Child.

Who would not weep seeing the Mother of Christ in such agony?

Who would not feel compassion on seeing Christ's mother suffering with her Son?

She saw Jesus in torment and subjected to the scourge for the sins of his people.

She saw her own dear Son dying, abandoned, as he gave up his spirit.

O Mother, fountain of love, make me feel the power of sorrow, that I may mourn with you.

Let my heart burn in the love of Christ my Lord, that I may be pleasing to him.

Holy Mother, may the wounds of the Crucified go deep into my heart.

Share with me the sufferings of your Son who suffered for me.

Let me sincerely weep with you, grieving the Crucified, for as long as I live.

I desire to stand beside the cross with you, and gladly share the weeping.

Chosen Virgin of virgins, do not turn away from me, let me mourn with you.

Let me bear the death of Christ, share in his Passion, and commemorate his wounds.

Let me be wounded with his wounds, inebriated by the cross because of love for the Son.

Lest I burn in the flames, may I be defended by you, Virgin, on the day of judgment.

Let me be protected by the cross, strengthened by Christ's death, cherished by grace.

When my body dies, may my soul be given the glory of paradise. Amen.

Brother Joel Giallanza, C.S.C., has served in administration and formation on various levels for the Congregation of Holy Cross. He has directed retreats on spirituality, religious life, and scripture in the United States and throughout the world. Brother Joel currently serves as Vicar for Religious, and Coordinator for the Institute for Spiritual Direction, a formation program for spiritual directors, for the Diocese of Austin, Texas. He is the author of *Questions Jesus Asked: Provisions for the Spiritual Journey* and *Source and Summit: Six Great Spiritual Guides Talk about the Eucharist*.